SCIENCE

OF

VEDIC METRES AND MUSICAL NOTES

By

Prof. Ravi Prakash Arya

Amazon Books, USA

In association with

Indian Foundation for Vedic Science

1051, Sector-1, Rohtak, Haryana, India Pin124001
Ph. No. 09313033917; 09650183260
Email: vedicscience@gmail.com; vedicscience@rediffmail.com
Web: https://vedic-sciences.com

First Edition

Kali era : 5119 (c. 2018)
Kalpa era: 1,97,29,49,119
Brahma era: 15,55,21,97,29,49,119

ISBN 81- 87710-32-2

THE Veda is the science of cosmology dealing with creation involving all its three aspects viz. adhibhautika (physical or geophysical aspect), adhidaivika (astronomical or astrophysical aspect) and adhyātmika (metaphysical or spiritual aspect). The Bhagvadgītā (2.45) amply announces this character of the Veda as:

त्रैगुण्यविषया वेदा ।
traiguṇyaviṣayā vedā

[Meaning] The Vedas deal with the creation evolving out of the three Guṇas (sattva, rajas and tamas) of Prakṛti.

These scientific mysteries of creation were unfolded through a scientific mode of documentation variously classified as ṛcās, yajuṣas and sāmans. The documentation in the form of ṛcās was known as the *Ṛgveda*, documentation in the form of yajuṣas was called as the Yajurveda and similarly documentation in the form of sāmans was known as the Sāmaveda. The technique and methodology of documenting the science of universal creation were also based on laws of universal creation. It is often quoted in the Vedic tradition that the documentation of the science of creation in the form of ṛcās was based on agni, i.e. geothermal energy. Agni (geothermal energy is called as a dominant factor of Bhūloka planets like earth. According to the Nirukta (7.5), Agni (geothermal energy) is related to earth[1]. The documentation of science of creation in the form of yajuṣas was based upon Vāyu (field energy existing into

[1] अग्निपृथिवीस्थानः A *agniḥ pṛthivi sthānaḥ*

the intermediate space). According to the Nirukta (7.5), the Vāyu (Air) as energy is located in the intermediate space[1]. The documentation of science of creation in the form of sāmans was based upon Sūrya (solar energy) existing in the celestial space. According to the Nirukta (7.5), Sūrya (solar energy) is located in the celestial or light space[2].

Not only the Nirukta, but the Śatapatha Brāhmaṇa (11.5.8.3) also sheds an ample good light on the composition of the *Ṛgveda*, the Yajurveda and the Sāmaveda. Accordingly, above mentioned three the Vedas came into existence on account of three forms of energy, i.e. the *Ṛgveda* came into being on account of Agni (geothermal energy), the Yajurveda came into being on account of Vāyu (air energy) and on account of Sūrya (solar energy) came into being the Sāmaveda.[1] The author of this Brāhmaṇa describes energy by the word tapta as:

तेभ्यस्तप्तेभ्यस्त्रयो वेदाऽजायन्त।
अग्नेर्ऋग्वेदो वायोर्यजुर्वेदः सूर्यात्सामवेदः।

tebhyastaptebhyastrayo vedā ajāyanta.
agner ṛgvedo vāyor yajurvedaḥ sūryātsāmavedaḥ.

From three energies originated three the Vedas. From Agni (geothermal or observer space energy originated the *Ṛgveda*, from the field the Yajurveda, from the solar

---

1 वायवेन्द्रो वान्तरिक्षस्थानः *vāyavendro vāntrikṣasthānaḥ*

2 तेभ्यस्तप्तेभ्यस्त्रयो वेदाऽजायन्त।
अग्नेर्ऋग्वेदो वायोर्यजुर्वेदः सूर्यात्सामवेदः।
tebhyastaptebhyastrayo vedā ajāyanta.
agner ṛgvedo vāyor yajurvedaḥ sūryātsāmavedaḥ.

energy or light the Sāmaveda.

The Manusmṛti also speaks the same language while dealing with the origin of the Vedas. According to Manusmṛti, 'Agni (geothermal energy), Vāyu (field energy) and Sūrya (solar energy) are the main instruments behind the Yajña (the process of creation). The *Ṛgveda*, the Yajurveda and the Sāmaveda originated on account of these energies[1].

The Gopatha Brāhmaṇa also associates Agni (geothermal energy/observer space energy) to the Bhūloka (earth/observer space), Vāyu (field energy) to the Antarikṣa-loka (intermediate space) and Sūrya (solar energy/light) to the Dyuloka (celestial sphere/light space). Thus the whole creation on the earth gets summed up between the earth, the sun and intervened by the intermediate space and the whole cosmic creation gets summed up between light space and observer space intervened by the intermediate space. The other way round we can say that the earth and the sun are interdependent for the creation on the earth. Keeping in view of this fact, the Vedas use the word dyāvā-pṛthivī time and again as a Devatā Dvandva compound. In fact, the interaction of solar energy with the geothermal energy causes the origin of life on the earth. This interaction is possible due to earth's revolution around the sun. Thus the Yajña (the process of creation) on the earth is going on due to joint participation of the earth

---

1 अग्निवायुरविभ्यस्तुत्रयं ब्रह्मसनातनम् ।
दुदोहयज्ञसिघ्यर्थं ऋग्यजुसामलक्षणम् ।
agni vāyu ravibhyastu trayaṁ brahma sanātanam
dudoha yajña-siddyarthaṁ ṛgyajuḥsāmalakṣaṇam.

and the sun.

When the earth moves around the sun, Sun's position in relation to Earth changes with the change of every solar month (represented by a Saṅkrānti). The sun describes seven great circles of latitude on the earth during 12 months of a year. These seven great circles of latitude described by the sun are known as the seven major chhandas. The seven great circles of latitude or chhandas described by the sun on the earth are as follows:

23.5^0 circle of latitude south of equator known as Tropic of Capricorn or the Gāyatrī Chhanda is caused by the sun when it transits through Makara (Capricorn) sign on 22nd December. This solar month is known in the Vedas as Aruṇa month.

The second circle of latitude described by the sun is 20^0 south of the equator. This circle is known in the Vedas as the uṣṇika chhanda. It is caused by the sun during its transit through Kumbha and Dhanu signs on 21st January and 22nd Nov. respectively. The solar months formed on this chhanda are known in the Vedas as Aruṇarāja and Sambhara months.

The third circle of latitude described by the sun is 12^0 south of the equator. This circle is known in the Vedas as the Anuṣṭup chhanda. It is caused by the sun during its transit through the Mīna and the Vṛścika signs on 20th Feb and 23rd Oct. respectively. The solar months formed on this chhanda are known in the Vedas as Puṇḍarika and Sarvauṣāḍha months.

The fourth circle of latitude described by the sun is 0^0 equator. This circle is known in the Vedas as the Bṛhati chhanda. It is caused by the sun during its transit through the Meṣa and Tulā signs on 21st March and 23rd Sept. respectively. The solar months formed on this chhanda are known in the Vedas as Viśvajita and Irāvān months.

The fifth circle of latitude described by the sun is 12^0 north of the equator. This circle is known in the Vedas as the Paṅkti chhanda. It is caused by the sun during its transit through the Vṛṣabha and the Kanyā signs on 21st April and 23rd August respectively. The solar months formed on this chhanda are known in the Vedas as Abhijita and Rasavān.

The sixth circle of latitude described by the sun is 20^0 north of the equator. This circle is known in the Vedas as the Triṣṭup chhanda. It is caused by the sun during its transit through the Mithuna and the Siṅha signs on 22nd May and 23rd July respectively. The solar months formed on this chhanda are known in the Vedas as Ārdrā and Unnavān months.

The seventh circle of latitude described by the sun is 23.5^0 north of the equator. This circle is known in the Vedas as the Jagati chhanda. It is caused by the sun during its transit through the Karka sign on 22nd June. Thc solar month formed on this chhanda is known in the Vedas as Pinvamāna month.

The process of describing seven chhandas is known in the Vedas as Vedī parigraha (Enclosing of the earth). In fact, this enclosure of the sun on the earth is known as chhanda. Etymologically also chhanda means enclosure: chandāŠsi chādanāt.

The Yajurveda (1.26) describes sun's power of

gravitation. The sun is gravitating the earth and encloses the earth with hundreds and thousands of rays.

देव सवितः परमस्यां पृथिव्यां शतेन पाशैः ॥

deva savitaḥ paramasyāṁ pṛthivyāṁ śatena pāśaiḥ //

In the next Mantra (*Yajurveda*: 1.27), three different enclosures of the sun on the south, west and north of earth have been respectively described as Gāyatrī, Triṣṭubha and Jagati chhanda.

गायत्रेण त्वा छन्दसा परिगृह्णामि
त्रैष्टुभेन त्वा छन्दसा परिगृह्णामि
जागतेन त्वा छन्दसा परिगृह्णामि ।

gāyatreṇa tvā chhandasā parigṛhṇāmi
traiṣṭubhena tvā chhandasā parigṛhṇāmi
jāgatena tvā chhandasā parigṛhṇāmi /

The Śatapatha Brāhmaṇa (1.2.5.1-13) gives a detailed commentary on this Mantra of the Yajurveda and illustrates a ritual of the Vedī Parigraha (enclosing the Altar/earth). The ritual in the Śatapatha Brāhmaṇa reads as under:

देवाश्च वा असुराश्च उभये प्रजापत्याः पस्पृधिरे। ततो देवा अनुव्यमिवासुः। अथ हासुरा मेनिरे अस्माकमेवेदं खलु भुवनमिति ॥1 ॥

devāścha vā asurāścha ubhaye prajāpatyāḥ paspṛdhire / tato devā anuvyamivāsuḥ / atha hāsurā menire asmākamevedaṁ khalu bhuvanamiti //1 //

सायण भाष्य- इत्थं स्तम्बयजुर्हरणं विधाय वेदिपरिग्रहं वक्तुमितिहासमुपन्यस्यति-देवाश्चेति। 'पस्पृधिरे' सपर्द्धां कृतवन्तः। 'अपस्पृधेथामानृचुरानृहुः (पासु. 6.1.36) इति सम्प्रसारणनिपातनस्योपलक्षणत्वमभिप्रेत्य लिट्यपि सम्प्रसारणं कृतम। सपर्द्धमानानां तेषां मध्ये 'देवाः' 'ततः' तेभ्योऽसुरेभ्यः 'अनुव्यम' अनुगमनं न्यग्भूतिं प्राप्ता इव बभूवुः। 'अथ ह' अनन्तरमेव तेऽसुरा मन्यन्ते स्म। किमिति? 'इदम' सर्वं जगदस्माकमेवेति।

Sāyaṇa Bhāṣya- itthaṁ stambayajurharaṇaṁ vidhāya

vediparigrahaṁ vaktumitihāsamupanyasyati-devāścheti । 'paspṛdhire' saparddhāṁ kṛtavantaḥ । 'apaspṛdhethāmānṛchurānṛhuḥ (pāsu. 6.1.36) iti samprasāraṇanipātanasyopalakṣaṇatvamabhipretya liṭyapi samprasāraṇaṁ kṛtama । saparddhamānānāṁ teṣāṁ madhye 'devāḥ' 'tataḥ' tebhyo'surebhyaḥ 'anuvyama' anugamanaṁ nyagbhūtiṁ prāptā iva babhūvuḥ । 'atha ha' anantarameva te'surā manyante sma । kimiti? 'idama' sarvaṁ jagadasmākameveti ।

Having described the ritual of stamba-yaju-haraṇa (symbolising the dissipation the forces of darkness that are anti-creation forces, the ritual of 'Altar enclosing' representing various circles of latitude described by the sun along the earth are depicted here through a method of historical narration of the natural phenomenon.

The forces of light (instrumental in creation) and the forces of the darkness (anti-creation forces) both having originated from Prajāpati (natural phenomenon of the rotation of the earth on its axis and its revolution around the sun), contended for superiority. In this contention for superiority, the forces of light (pro-creation forces) seemed to have been defeated by the forces of darkness. Since then the forces of darkness thought that this world belonged to them.

ते होचुः –हन्तेमा पृथिवीं विभजामहै तां विभज्योपजीवामेति। तामौक्ष्णैश्चर्म्मभिः पश्चात् प्राञ्चो विभजमाना अभीयुः ॥2 ॥

te hochuḥ - hantemā pṛthivīṁ vibhajāmahai, tāṁ vibhajyopajīvāmeti । tāmaukṣaṇaiścharmmabhiḥ paśchāt prācho vibhajamānā abhīyuḥ ॥2 ॥

सायण भाष्य - एवमुक्त्वा किमुक्तवन्त इति तद्दर्शयति-ते हेति। 'हन्त' इति हर्षे। यत एवं देवा न्यग्भूताः, अतो न्ष्रित्यूहं वयम् 'इमाम' पृथिवीं विभजामहै। विभज्य च तां यथाभागमुपजीवामेति। एवमुक्त्वा किं कृतवन्त इति तदाह-तामिति। 'औक्ष्णैः' उक्ष्णोऽन्डुहःसम्बन्धिभिश्चर्म्मभिः। उक्षन्-शब्दात् 'तस्ये-दम' (पासू. 4.3.120) इत्यणि

'षपूर्वहन्धृतराज्ञाम्' (पासू. 6.4.135) इत्यलोपः। तैश्चर्मभिः 'पश्चात्' प्रतीचीं दिशमारम्य 'प्राञ्चः' प्राङ्मुखाविभजमानः 'अभीयुः' अभिजग्मुरित्यर्थः॥ 2 ॥

Sāyaṇa Bhāṣya - ēvamuktvā kimuktavanta iti taddarśayati-te heti / 'hanta' iti harṣe / yata ēvaṁ devā nyagbhūtāḥ, ato nṣprityūhaṁ vayam 'imāma' pṛthivīṁ vibhajāmahai / vibhajya cha tāṁ yathābhāgamupajīvāmeti / ēvamuktvā kiṁ kṛtavanta iti tadāha-tāmiti / 'aukṣaṇaiḥ' ukṣaṇo'nḍuhaḥsambandhibhiścharmmabhiḥ / ukṣan-śabdāt 'tasye-dama' (pāsū. 4.3.120) ityaṇi 'ṣapūrvahandhṛtarājñām' (pāsū. 6.4.135) ityalopaḥ / taiścharmabhiḥ 'paśchāt' pratīchīṁ diśamāramya 'prāchaḥ' prāṅmukhāvibhajamānaḥ 'abhīyuḥ' abhijagmurityarthaḥ // 2 //

The forces of darkness, being in dominant position, said, 'Let us share the earth among us and having done so, let us subsist upon it.' They set about sharing it with ox-hide from west to east.

NB: In the Indian context, after the rise of the sun in the east, there will be light east through west and the darkness will prevail from west to east. So it has been said that the forces of darkness set about sharing the earth from west to east.

तद्वै देवाः शुश्रुवुः विभजन्ते ह वा इमामसुराः पृथिवीम् प्रेत तदेष्यामो यत्रेमामसुरा विभजन्त, के ततः स्याम यदस्यै न भजेमहीति। ते यज्ञमेव विष्णुं पुरस्कृत्येयुः। **3**।

tadvai devāḥ śuśruvuḥ vibhajante ha vā imāmasurāḥ pṛthivīm, preta tadeṣyāmo yatremāmasurā vibhajanta, ke tataḥ syāma yadasyai na bhajemahīti **/** *te yajñameva viṣṇuṁ puraskṛtyeyuḥ* **/** *3* **/**

सायण भाष्य - असुरेष्वेवं कृतवत्सु देवाः किं कृतवन्त इति तदाह-तद्वा इति। प्रेतत्यादि। अस्माकं तूष्णीमवस्थानमनुचितम्, अस्माभिरपि तद्विषये प्रयतितव्यमिति, परस्परमभिमुखीकृत्येत्यर्थः प्रतिपाद्यते- हे देवाः ! यूयं 'प्रेत' गच्छत, प्रोत्सहध्वमिति यावत्। यस्मिन्स्थानेऽसुराः पृथिवीं विभजन्ते, तत्स्थानं गमिष्यामः। गत्वा च 'यत्' यदि

'अस्यै' षष्ठ्यर्थे चतुर्थी (पासू. 2.3.62। वा0 1509) 'अस्याः' पृथिव्याः सम्बन्धि स्थानं न प्राप्नुयामः, ('ततः' तर्हिवयमभागिने भवेम; यदि तु प्राप्नुयामः तदा) भागिनः 'स्याम' भवेमेत्यर्थः। एवमालोच्य देवैः कृतं दर्शयति-त इति। यज्ञातमकमेव 'विष्णुम्' पुरतो धारयित्वा 'ईयुः' गतवन्त इत्यर्थः ॥ 3 ॥

Sāyaṇa Bhāṣya - asureṣvevaṁ kṛtavatsu devāḥ kiṁ kṛtavanta iti tadāha-tadvā iti / pretatyādi / asmākaṁ tūṣṇīmavasthānamanuchitam, asmābhirapi tadviṣaye prayatitavyamiti, parasparamabhimukhīkṛtyetyarthaḥ pratipādyate- he devāḥ! yūyaṁ 'preta' gachchhata, protsahadhvamiti yāvat /yasminsthāne'surāḥ pṛthivīṁ vibhajante, tatsthānṁ gamiṣyāmaḥ / gatvā cha 'yat' yadi 'asyai' ṣaṣṭhyarthe chaturthī (pāsū. 2.3.62 / vā0 1509) 'asyāḥ' pṛthivyāḥ sambandhi sthānṁ na prāpnuyāmaḥ, ('tataḥ' tarhivayamabhāgine bhavema; yadi tu prāpnuyāmaḥ tadā) bhāginḥ 'syāma' bhavemetyarthaḥ / ēvamālochya devaiḥ kṛtaṁ darśayati-ta iti / yajñātamakameva 'viṣṇum' purato dhārayitvā 'īyuḥ' gatavanta ityarthaḥ // 3 //

The forces of the light (pro-creation forces) heard this and thought, 'The forces of darkness are actually dominating this earth. Let us go to the place where the forces of darkness are sharing the earth. What would become of us if we were deprived of our share? With the Viṣṇu (the sun) as their head, they went there.'

ते होचुः-अनु नोऽस्यां पृथिव्यामाभजत, अस्त्वेव नोऽप्यस्यां भाग इति। ते हासुरा असूयन्त इवोचुः - यावदेवैष विष्णुरभिशेते, तावद्वो दद्म इति ॥ 4 ॥

te hochuḥ-anu no'syāṁ pṛthivyāmabhajata, astveva no'pyasyāṁ bhāga iti / te hāsurā asūyanta ivochuḥ - yāvadevaiṣa viṣṇurabhiśete, tāvadvo dadma iti // 4 //

सायण भाष्य-गत्वा चासुरान् प्रति किमुक्तवन्त इति तदाह—ते हेति। 'अस्याम्' पृथिव्याम् 'नः' अस्माकमप्यस्यां भागो भवत्विति। असुरैः कृतं प्रतिवचनं दर्शयति-ते हेति। 'असूयन्त इव' असूयां कुर्वन्त इव, असहमाना इति यावत्। यावन्तं देशं विष्णुर्व्याप्य वर्तते, तत्परिमाणं स्थानं युष्मभ्यं प्रयच्छाम इति॥ 4॥

Sāyaṇa Bhāṣya-gatvā chāsurān prati kimuktavanta iti, tadāha-te heti / 'asyām' pṛthivyām 'nḥ' asmākamapyasyāṁ bhāgo bhavatviti / asuraiḥ kṛtaṁ prativachanṁ darśayati-te heti / 'asūyanta iva' asūyāṁ kurvanta iva, asahamānā iti yāvat / yāvantaṁ deśaṁ viṣṇurvyāpya vartate, tatparimāṇaṁ sthānaṁ yuṣmabhyaṁ prayachchhāma iti // 4 //

They then said to the anti-creation forces of darkness, 'We may also be included in sharing the earth. Let there also be our share in it. The anti-creation forces of darkness could not tolerate it and told, 'As much place as this Viṣṇu (the sun) occupies through its circles of latitude (chhandas) on the earth, let only that much be yours.' Meaning to say, from 23.5^{0} north to 23.5^{0} south of the earth, the Viṣṇu (the sun) is visible. Rest of the parts remains in darkness.

वामनो ह विष्णुरास। तद्देवा न जिहीडिरे-महद्वैनोऽदुर्य नो यज्ञसम्मितमदुरिति ॥5॥

vāmano ha viṣṇurāsa / taddevā na jihīḍire-mahadvai no'durya no yajñasammitamaduriti // 5 //

सायण भाष्य-असुरैरभिहिते देवास्तदंगीचक्रुरित्याह-वामनो हेति। विष्णुर्हि तदानीम् 'वामन्:' खर्वो बभूव। अत एवासुरास्तेनाक्रान्तं स्थानं प्रयच्छाम इत्यब्रुवन्। अथापि 'तत्' असुरैरुक्तं देवाः; 'न जिहीडिरे' न ह्यनादृतं चक्रुः किन्त्वाद्रियन्ते स्मेत्यर्थः। 'हेड्ट अनादरे' (भ्वा0 आ0 285) इति धातुः। आदरण प्रकारमाह-महदिति। विष्णुर्हि यज्ञः, अतो 'यज्ञसम्मितम्' स्थानमस्मभ्यं दत्तवन्त इति यत्, तत् 'नः' अस्माकम् 'महत्' अधिकम्॥

Sāyaṇa Bhāṣya-asurairabhihite devāstadaṁgīchakrurityāha-vāmano heti / viṣṇurhi tadānīm 'vāmanḥ' kharvo babhūva / ata ēvāsurāstenākrāntaṁ sthānaṁ prayachchhāma ityabruvan / athāpi 'tat' asurairuktaṁ devāḥ; 'na jihīḍire' na hyanādṛtaṁ chakruḥ kintvādriyante smetyarthaḥ / 'heḍṛ anādare' (Bhvā. Ā. 285) iti dhātuḥ / ādaraṇa prakāramāha-mahaditi / viṣṇurhi yajñaḥ, ato 'yajñasammitam' sthānamasmabhyaṁ dattavanta iti yat, tat 'naḥ' asmākam 'mahat' adhikam //

Viṣṇu's (sun's) area on the earth (from 23.5° North to 23.5° South of equator) is very short. The forces of light, however, had no objection and accepted this proposal. 'Give us as much as is required for the Yajña (creation on earth), that will be sufficient for us.' said the forces of light. Thus from 23.5° North to 23.5° South of equator became the part of the forces of light and rest became the part of forces of darkness.

ते प्राञ्चं विष्णुं निपाद्य छन्दोभिरभितः पर्यगृह्णन्-'गायत्रेण त्वा छन्दसा परिगृह्णामि'-(1.27) इति, दक्षिणतः। 'त्रैष्टुभेन त्वा छन्दसा परिगृह्णामि'-(1.27) इति, पश्चात्। ''जागतेन त्वा छन्दसा परिगृह्णामि'- (1.27) इति, उत्तरतः ॥ 6 ॥

te prāñcham viṣṇum nipādya chhandobhirabhitaḥ paryagṛhṇan- 'gāyatreṇa tvā chhandasā parigṛhṇāmi'-(1.27) iti, dakṣiṇataḥ I 'traiṣṭubhena tvā chhandasā parigṛhṇāmi'-(1.27) iti, paśchāt I ''jāgatena tvā chhandasā parigṛhṇāmi'- (1.27) iti, uttarataḥ II 6 II

सायण भाष्य - एवं विचार्य देवैः कृतं दर्शयति-त इति। यज्ञातमकम् 'विष्णुम्' 'प्राञ्चं' प्राक्शिरसं निपात्य (द्य) दक्षिणतः, पश्चात्, उत्तरतश्च गाय□त्र्यादिच्छन्दोभिः सर्वतः पर्यगृह्णन् ॥ 6 ॥

sāyaṇa bhāṣya - ēvaṁ vichārya devaiḥ kṛtaṁ darśayati-ta iti I yajñātamakam 'viṣṇum' 'prāñcham' prākśirasaṁ nipātya (dya) dakṣiṇataḥ, paśchāt, uttarataścha gāyayādichchhandobhiḥ sarvataḥ paryagṛhṇan II 6 II

The forces of light having laid down Viṣṇu, the sun on the eastward enclosed earth by various chhandas; 23¼° south of the equator was enclosed with the Gāyatrī chhanda with the Yajurvedic Mantra, 'I enclose you by the Gāyatrī chhanda' (VS.1.27). Henceforth the Tropic of the Capricorn is denoted by the Gāyatrī metre. (Note: the Gāyatrī metre has 24 syllables to denote 23¼°). The western side with the Triṣṭup chhanda with the recitation of the Mantra, 'I enclose you with the help of Triṣṭup chhanda' (VS.1.27). Triṣṭubh being the next to Jagatī from west to east. The northern side with the Jagatī chhanda. 'I enclose you with the help of the Jagati chhanda' (VS.1.27). The tropic of cancer is denoted by the Jagatī metre. The Jagatī metre has 48 syllables, the double of 24 to represent 23¼° N+23¼° S.

तं छन्दोभिरभितः परिगृह्य, अग्निं पुरस्तात् समाधाय, तेनार्चन्तः श्राम्यन्तश्चेरुः। तेनेमां सर्वां पृथिवीं समविन्दन्त। तद् यदेनेनेमां सर्वां समविन्दन्त तस्माद्वेदिर्नाम। तस्मादाहुः-यावती वेदिः तावती पृथिवीति-एतया हीमां सवांर्समविन्दन्त। एवं ह वा इमां सर्वां सपत्नानां संवृंक्ते। निर्भजत्यस्यै सपत्नान्-य एवमेतद्वेद ॥ 7 ॥

taṁ chhandobhirabhitaḥ parigṛhya, agniṁ purastāt samādhāya, tenārchantaḥ śrāmyantaścheruḥ I tenemāṁ sarvāṁ pṛthivīṁ samavindanta I tad yadenenemāṁ sarvāṁ samavindanta, tasmādvedirnāma I tasmādāhuḥ-yāvatī vediḥ, tāvatī pṛthivīti-ētayā hīmāṁ savāṁrsamavindanta I ēvaṁ ha vā imāṁ sarvāṁ sapatnānāṁ saṁvṛṁkte I nirbhajatyasyai sapatnān-ya ēvametadveda II 7 II

सायण भाष्य - तमिति। 'तम्' विष्णुं गाय□यादिभिश्छन्दोभिः सर्वतःपरिगृह्य पूर्वस्यां दिशि-आहवनीयाख्यम् 'अग्निम्' प्रज्वाल्य, 'तेन्' विष्ण्वात्मकेन् यज्ञेन् 'अर्चन्तः' पूजयन्तः, 'श्राम्यन्तः' कर्मानुष्ठानजनितं श्रमं प्राप्नुवन्तः 'चेरुः' पूर्ववद्ववृतिरे। चरित्वा च 'तेन्' यज्ञात्मकस्य विष्णोराधारभूतेन् स्थानेन देवाः सर्वामेवेमां पृथिवीं सम्यागलभन्त। अतो विद्यते लभ्यते अनेनेति यज्ञस्थानस्य 'वेदि' नामधेयम् निर्वक्ति - तद्यदिति। उक्तं वेद्याः सर्वपृथिवीलाभरूपत्वम्, इदानीं वेदिपृथिव्योस्तादातम्यविषयामभियुक्त-प्रसिद्धिमुदाहरति - तस्मादिति। यत्परिमाणविशिष्टा खलु वेदिः, तत्परिमाणैव पृथिवी कुत इत्यत आह-एतयेति। 'हि' यस्मात् 'एतया' वेद्या इमां सर्वां पृथिवीमलभन्त, अतस्तल्लाभहेतुत्वात् ततोऽनन्येत्यर्थः। इत्थं पुरावृत्तमुदाहृत्य प्रकृते योजयति-एवं हेति। यथैव हि वेदिपरिग्रहाद्देवा असुरसकाशात् कृतस्नां पृथिवीमपहृतवन्तः, एवमेवायं यजमानोऽपि शत्रुसम्बन्धिनीं सर्वां भूमिमपहरति। तांश्च शत्रून् 'अस्याः' पृथिव्याः 'र्न्भिजति' निर्भक्तान् भागरहितान् करोतीत्यर्थः। तस्माद्गायत्रेणेत्यादिभिर्मन्त्रैः स्□येन वेदिं दक्षिणतः पश्चादुत्तरतश्च रेखया परिगृह्णीयादित्यर्थः ॥7 ॥

Sāyaṇa Bhāṣya- tamiti I 'taṁ' viṣṇuṁ

gāyatryādibhiśchhandobhiḥ sarvataḥparigṛhya, pūrvasyāṁ diśi-āhavanīyākhyam 'agnmi' prajvālya, 'ten' viṣṇvātmaken yajñen 'archantaḥ' pūjayantaḥ, 'śrāmyantaḥ' karmānuṣṭhānajanitaṁ śramaṁ prāpnuvantaḥ 'cheruḥ' pūrvavadvavṛtire I charitvā cha 'ten' yajñātmakasya viṣṇorādhārabhūten sthānena devāḥ sarvāmevemāṁ pṛthivīṁ samyāgalabhanta I ato vidyate labhyate aneneti yajñasthānasya 'vedi' nāmadheyam nirvakti - tadyaditi I uktaṁ vedyāḥ sarvapṛthivīlābharūpatvam, idānīṁ vedipṛthivyostādātamyaviṣayāmabhiyukta- prasiddhimudāharati - tasmāditi I yatparimāṇaviśiṣṭā khalu vediḥ, tatparimāṇaiva pṛthivī kuta ityata āha-ētayeti I 'hi' yasmāt 'ētayā' vedyā imāṁ sarvāṁ pṛthivīmalabhanta, atastallābhahetutvāt tato'nanyetyarthaḥ I itthaṁ purāvṛttamudāhṛtya prakṛte yojayati-ēvaṁ heti I yathaiva hi vediparigrahāddevā asurasakāśāt kṛtasnāṁ pṛthivīmapahṛtavantaḥ, ēvamevāyaṁ yajamāno'pi śatrusambandhinīṁ sarvāṁ bhūmimapaharati I tāṁścha śatrūn 'asyāḥ' pṛthivyāḥ 'rnbhijati' nirbhaktān bhāgarahitān karotītyarthaḥ I tasmādgāyatreṇetyādibhirmantraiḥ śyena vediṁ dakṣiṇataḥ paśchāduttarataścha rekhayā parigṛhṇīyādityarthaḥ II7 II

Having enclosed the earth on all the sides with various chhandas (metre-ranges) and having ignited the fire of creation (sun) known as the Āhavanīy fire on the east side, the forces of light went on performing their work of creation with this fire and they occupied the whole of the earth along the tropics. Because they occupied the whole earth for the process of creation, this earth came to be known as Vedī (occupied one) or the altar as we may call it in terms of the English language. That is the reason why it is often said that the earth has the same parameters as that of the Vedī, for the sake of creation the entire earth was occupied by the pro-creation forces. And so one can capture the entire earth from his rivals and can dispossess them of their share who realises this fact.

सोऽयं विष्णुर्ग्लानः छन्दोभिरभितः परिगृहीतः अग्निः पुरस्तात् नापक्रमणमास। स तत एवौषधीनां मूलान्युपमुम्लोच॥ 8 ॥

so'yaṁ viṣṇurglānaḥ, chhandobhirabhitaḥ parigṛhītaḥ, agniḥ purastāt nāpakramaṇamāsa I sa tata ēvauṣadhīnāṁ mūlānyupamumlocha II 8 II

सायण भाष्य - अथ वेदेः खननं विधित्सुः प्रकृतमितिहासशेषमनक्रामति-सोऽयमिति। 'सः' यज्ञात्मको 'विष्णुः' दक्षिणतः पश्चादुत्तरतश्च छन्दोभिः परिगृहीतत्वात् पूर्वस्यां दिशि चाग्नेरवस्थानादितस्ततश्चलितुमशक्यतवेन 'ग्लानः' श्रान्तः सन् अपक्रमणम् अपगमनम् 'नास' न जगाम। 'अस गतिदीप्तयादानेषु'-(भ्वा0 उ0 911)-इत्यस्माल्लिटि रूपम्। यद्वा-अस्तेरेव लिटिच्छान्दसो भूभावाऽभावः। ग्लानस्य तस्य विष्णोरपगमनं न बभूवेत्यर्थः। स च सर्वतः परिगृहीतो विष्णुः 'तत एव' तस्मिन्नेव स्थाने- ओषधीनां मूलान्युपेत्य भूम्यन्तर्गतः सन् 'मुम्लोच' अस्तंगतः, अदृश्योबभूव ॥ 8 ॥

Sāyaṇa Bhāṣya - atha vedeḥ khananaṁ vidhitsuḥ prakṛtamitihāsaśeṣamanakrāmati-so'yamiti I 'saḥ' yajñātmako 'viṣṇuḥ' dakṣiṇataḥ paśchāduttarataścha chhandobhiḥ parigṛhītatvāt pūrvasyāṁ diśi chāgneravasthānāditastataśchalitumaśakyatavena 'glānaḥ' śrāntaḥ san apakramaṇam' apagamanam 'nāsa' na jagāma I 'asa gatidīptayādāneṣu'-(Bhvā. U. 911)-ityasmālliṭi rūpam I yadvā-astereva liṭichchhāndaso bhūbhāvā'bhāvaḥ I glānasya tasya viṣṇorapagamanaṁ na babhūvetyarthaḥ I sa cha sarvataḥ parigṛhīto viṣṇuḥ 'tata ēva' tasminneva sthāne- ōṣadhīnāṁ mūlānyupetya bhūmyantargataḥ san 'mumlocha' astaṁgataḥ, adṛśyobabhūva II 8 II

The Viṣṇu (sun) was bounded on all directions by the metres, with his head on the east direction. Thus unable to escape anywhere beyond tropical encompassment, i.e. beyond 23¼° north and south of the equator (tropical zone), the Sun moved down to the roots of the vegetation.

ते ह देवा ऊचुः - क्व नु विष्णुरभूत् क्व नु यज्ञोऽभूदिति। ते होचुः- छन्दोभिरभितः परिगृहीतः, अग्निः पुरस्तात्, नापक्रमणमस्ति; अत्रैवान्विच्छतेति। तं खनन्त इवान्वीषुः तं □यंगुलेऽन्वविन्दन्। तस्मात् यंगुला वेदिः स्यात्। तदु हापि पाचः □यंगुलामेव सौम्यस्याध्वरस्य वेदिं चक्रे ॥ 9 ॥

te ha devā ūchuḥ - kva nu viṣṇurabhūt, kva nu yajño'bhūditi | te hochuḥ- chhandobhirabhitaḥ parigṛhītaḥ, agniḥ purastāt, nāpakramaṇamasti; atraivānvichchhateti | taṁ khananta ivānvīṣuḥ taṁ yaṁgule'nvavindan | tasmāt yaṁgulā vediḥ syāt | tadu hāpi pāchaḥ yaṁgulāmeva saumyasyādhvarasya vediṁ chakre || 9 ||

सायण भाष्य - अनन्तरं च ते देवास्तत्र विष्णुमपश्यन्तो वितर्कितवन्तः, किमित्याह-ते ह देवा इति। विष्णुः 'क्व' कुत्राभूत्? तदात्मको यज्ञश्च क्व वाऽभूदिति। एवं वितर्क्य तैर्निर्णीतमर्थं दर्शयति-ते होचुरिति। अत्रैवेति। चतसृष्वपि दिक्षु परिवृतत्वेन गमनासम्भवात् 'अत्रैव' स्थाने तस्य विष्णोरन्वेषणं कुरुतेत्यर्थः। इत्थं परस्परं निश्चित्य भूमिं खनन्त इव 'तम्' विष्णुमन्विष्टवन्तः। अन्विष्य तं भूम्यन्तस्□यंगुले 'अन्वविन्दन्' अलभन्त। यत एवम्, अत इदानीमपि यज्ञलाभाय वेदेस्□यंगुलखननमृषिसंवादेन द्रढयति-तदु हेति। 'पाचः' नाम कश्चित्, स खलु सोमयागस्यापि वेदिं □यंगुलखातामेव कृतवान्। अतोऽत्रापि □यंगुलखाता वेदिर्युक्तेति भावः ॥ 9 ॥

Sāyaṇa Bhāṣya - anantaraṁ cha te devāstatra viṣṇumapaśyanto vitarkitavantaḥ, kimityāha-te ha devā iti | viṣṇuḥ 'kva' kutrābhūt? tadātmako yajñaścha kva vā'bhūditi | ēvaṁ vitarkya tairnirṇītamarthaṁ darśayati-te hochuriti | atraiveti | chatasṛṣvapi dikṣu parivṛtatvena gamanāsambhavāt 'atraiva' sthāne tasya viṣṇoranveṣaṇaṁ kurutetyarthaḥ | itthaṁ parasparaṁ niśchitya bhūmiṁ khananta iva 'tam' viṣṇumanviṣṭavantaḥ | anviṣya taṁ bhūmyantas yaṁgule 'anvavindan' alabhanta | yata ēvam, ata idānīmapi yajñalābhāya vedes yaṁgulakhananamṛṣisaṁvādena draḍhayati-tadu heti | 'pāchaḥ' nāma kaśchit, sa khalu somayāgasyāpi vediṁ yaṁgulakhātāmeva kṛtavān | ato'trāpi yaṁgulakhātā vediryukteti bhāvaḥ || 9 ||

The same narration is prolonged: The forces of light

said, 'What has become of Viṣṇu? What has become of the Yajña, the natural process of creation?' They said, 'Enclosed on all sides by metres, with its head towards the east on the equator, there is no way of escaping; search for the Viṣṇu went on here itself.' They searched for it by slightly digging the earth. They discovered it at a depth of three fingers, i.e they found that the Viṣṇu has moved down the earth three circles of latitude 120, 20° and 23.50 north and south of the equator. Therefore the Vedī (altar) should be made three fingers deep. In view of the same fact, Pāñci named scholar made the earth three fingers deep.

तदु तथा न कुर्यात्। ओषधीनां वै स मूलान्युपाम्लोचत्-तस्मात्-ओषधीनामेव मूलान्युच्छेत्तवै ब्रूयात्। यन्वेवात्र विष्णुमन्वविन्दन्-तस्माद्वेदिर्नाम ॥10 ॥

tadu tathā na kuryāt I ōṣadhīnāṁ vai samūlānyupāmlochat-tasmāt-ōṣadhīnāmeva mūlānyuchchhettavai brūyāt I yannvevātra viṣṇumanvavindan-tasmādvedirnāma II10 II

सायण भाष्य - तामिमं पक्षं निषिध्य पक्षान्तरमाह-तदु तथेति। 'सः' विष्णुरोषधीनां खलु मूलान्युपेत्यान्तर्हितोऽभवत्। तस्माद् यावति देशे भूम्यामन्तरोषधीनां मूलानि प्रसरन्ति, तावत्पर्यन्तं खात्वा तन्मूलान्येवोच्छेत्तुं ब्रूयात्। 'तुमर्थे सेसेनः'- (पासू. 3.4.9)-इति तवैप्रत्ययः। पूर्वं कृत्स्नपृथिवीलाभहेतुतया वेदिनाम निरुक्तम, यज्ञात्मकस्य विष्णोर्लाभाधिकरणतयापि तन्निर्वक्ति-यन्नवेवेति।

Sāyaṇa Bhāṣya - tāmimaṁ pakṣaṁ niṣidhya pakṣāntaramāha-tadu tatheti I 'saḥ' viṣṇuroṣadhīnāṁ khalu mūlānyupetyāntarhito'bhavat I tasmād yāvati deśe bhūmyāmantaroṣadhīnāṁ mūlāni prasaranti, tāvatparyantaṁ khātvā tanmūlānyevochchhettuṁ brūyāt I 'tumarthe sesenaḥ'- (Pāsū. 3.4.9)- iti tavaipratyayaḥ I pūrvaṁ kṛtsnapṛthivīlābhahetutayā vedināma niruktama, yajñātmakasya viṣṇorlābhādhikaraṇatayāpi tannirvakti-yannaveveti I

But this should not be done. Since the Viṣṇu (Sun) moved the earth to the extent of the roots of the vegetations, so let him (the Adhvaryu) ask the Āgnidhra to cut out the roots of the vegetation, and because they found Viṣṇu in a Tropical region, so they called Tropics as an altar.

तमनुविद्योत्तरेण परिग्रहेण पर्यगृह्णन् - 'सूक्ष्मा चासि शिवा चासि'-(1.27) इति। दक्षिणत इमामेवैतत् पृथिवीं संविद्य सुक्ष्मां शिवामकुर्वत। 'स्योना चासि सुषदा चासि'-(1.27) इति। पश्चादिमामेवैतत् पृथिवीं संविद्य स्योनां सुषदामकुर्वत। 'ऊर्जास्वती चासि पयस्वती च-(1.27) इति। उत्तरत इमामेवैतत् पृथिवीं संविद्य रसवतीमुपजीवनीयामकुर्वत ॥ 11 ॥

tamanuvidyottareṇa parigraheṇa paryagṛhṇan - 'sūkṣamā chāsi śivā chāsi'-(1.27) iti / dakṣiṇata imāmevaitat pṛthivīṁ saṁvidya sukṣamāṁ śivāmakurvata / 'syonā chāsi suṣadā chāsi'-(1.27) iti / paśchādimāmevaitat pṛthivīṁ saṁvidya syonāṁ suṣadāmakurvata / 'ūrjāsvatī chāsi payasvatī cha'-(1.27) iti / uttarata imāmevaitat pṛthivīṁ saṁvidya rasavatīmupajīvanīyāmakurvata // 11 //

सायण भाष्य- अथ वेदेरुत्तरपरिग्रहः कर्तव्य इतीतिहासमुखेन विधिमुन्नयति-तमित्यादिना। 'तम्' विष्णुम्' अनुविद्य' लब्ध्वोत्तरपरिग्रहेण पर्यगृह्णन्। गायत्रेण त्वेत्यादिभिः प्राक् कृतः पूर्वपरिग्रहस्तदपेक्षयास्योत्तरत्वम्। तस्य स्वरूपमाह-सुक्ष्मा चासीत्यादिना। 'दक्षिणतः' वेदेर्दक्षिणस्यां दिशि 'सुक्ष्मा चासि'-इति यजुषा स्□येन लेखया परिगृह्णीयात्। मन्त्रतात्पर्यमाह - इमामिति। एवमुत्तरत्रापि योज्यम्। तृतीयमन्त्रे ऊर्क् शब्देन बलकरो रसो विवक्षित इति व्याचष्टे-रसवतीमिति। पयस्वतीत्यस्य व्याख्यानम्-उपजीवनीयामिति। पयस्विनी हि गौर्लोके-उपजीव्यते॥

Sāyaṇa Bhāṣya- atha vederuttaraparigrahaḥ kartavya itītihāsamukhena vidhimunnayati-tamityādinā / 'tam' viṣṇum' anuvidya' labdhvottaraparigraheṇa paryagṛhṇan / gāyatreṇa tvetyādibhiḥ prāk kṛtaḥ pūrvaparigrahastadapekṣayāsyottaratvam / tasya svarūpamāha-sukṣamā chāsītyādinā / 'dakṣiṇataḥ' vederdakṣiṇasyāṁ diśi 'sukṣamā chāsi'-iti yajuṣā śyena lekhayā parigṛhṇīyāt /

mantratātparyamāha - imāmiti । ēvamuttaratrāpi yojyam । tṛtīyamantre ūrk śabdena balakaro raso vivakṣita iti vyāchaṣṭe- rasavatīmiti । payasvatītyasya vyākhyānam- upajīvanīyāmiti । payasvinī hi gaurloke-upajīvyate ॥

Having found the Viṣṇu at the first cardinal point, i.e. 23¼° north and south of the equator, they enclosed him with a second enclosure, i.e at 20° north and south of the equator. On the north with the text (VS.1.27), 'You are of good soil and auspicious.' On the 20° south when the forces of light discovered Viṣṇu, they made the earth of good soil and auspicious. (The part of the earth around 20° south of the equator is fertile and auspicious). On the west it was enclosed with the text (VS.1.27), 'The pleasant and comfortable to sit upon are you.' Having thus located Viṣṇu on the west side of the earth, they made that part of the earth pleasant and comfortable to sit upon. On the 20° north the Viṣṇu was enclosed with the text (VS.1.27), 'Abounding in food and water are you.' Having discovered Viṣṇu on 20° north, they made part of the earth prosperous in food and water. (We can see the rivers originating from the north).

स वै त्रिः पूवंर् परिग्रहं परिगृह्णाति, त्रिरुत्तरम्। तत् षकृतवः, षड् वा ऋतवः संवत्सरस्य। संवत्सरो यज्ञः प्रजापतिः स यावानेव यज्ञो यावत्यस्य मात्रा तावन्तमेवैतत् परिगृह्णाति ॥ 12 ॥

sa vai triḥ pūvaṁr parigrahaṁ parigṛhṇāti, triruttaram । tat ṣaṭkṛtavaḥ, ṣaḍ vā ṛtavaḥ saṁvatsarasya । saṁvatsaro yajñaḥ prajāpatiḥ; sa yāvāneva yajño yāvatyasya mātrā tāvantamevaitat parigṛhṇāti ॥ 12 ॥

सायण भाष्य - पूर्वोत्तरपरिग्रहयोः संख्यां समुच्चित्य प्रशंसति - स वा इत्यादिना। षड्तुसमुदायात्मको यः संवत्सरः तदात्मकः प्रजापतिः संवत्सरकालभरणेन जातत्वादभेदोपचारः। आम्नास्यते ह्यग्रे बृहदारण्यके- 'तमेतावन्तं

कालमबिभर्यावान्तसंवत्सरस्तमेतावतः कालस्य परस्तादसृजत (1.2.4) इति। यज्ञश्चाऽऽश्रावयेत्यादिसप्तदशाक्षरसाध्यत्वात् 'एष वै सप्तदशः प्रजापतिर्यज्ञमन्वायत्तः'-(तैसं. 1.6.11) इति श्रुतेः प्रजापत्यात्मकः। एवम् 'सः' यज्ञः 'यावान्' यत्परिमाणविशिष्टः, 'अस्य' च यज्ञस्य 'मात्रा' परिमाणं च यावत्, तत्परिमाणविशिष्टमेवैतं यज्ञं षट्संख्यासंपादनेन 'परिगृह्णाति' स्वीकरोतीत्यर्थः ॥ 12 ॥

Sāyaṇa Bhāṣya - pūrvottaraparigrahayoḥ saṁkhyāṁ samuchchitya praśaṁsati - sa vā ityādinā I ṣaḍṛtusamudāyātmako yaḥ saṁvatsaraḥ, tadātmakaḥ prajāpatiḥ, saṁvatsarakālabharaṇena jātatvādabhedopachāraḥ I āmnāsyate hyagre bṛhadāraṇyake- 'tametāvantaṁ kālamabibharyāvāntasaṁvatsarastametāvataḥ kālasya parastādasṛjata' -(1.2.4) iti I yajñaśchā''śrāvayetyādisaptadaśākṣarasādhyatvāt 'ēṣa vai saptadaśaḥ prajāpatiryajñamanvāyattaḥ'-(taisaṁ. 1.6.11) iti śruteḥ prajāpatyātmakaḥ I ēvam 'saḥ' yajñaḥ 'yāvān' yatparimāṇaviśiṣṭaḥ, 'asya' cha yajñasya 'mātrā' parimāṇaṁ cha yāvat, tatparimāṇaviśiṣṭamevaitaṁ yajñaṁ ṣaṭsaṁkhyāsaṁpādanena 'parigṛhṇāti' svīkarotītyarthaḥ II 12 II

The Viṣṇu thus draws three enclosures before the equator, i.e. at the points of 23¼°, 20°, 12° south and three after the equator, i.e. 23¼°, 20°, 12° north of the equator. These all enclosures together make six. So are made the six seasons of the year. A year is the time process (Yajña) of creation (Prajāpati). As large is the yearly process of creation, so wide as its (tropical movement of the sun) extent is between the tropics. So, widely, he (the Adhvaryu) thereby encloses this fire altar.

षड्भिर्व्याहृतिभिः पूर्वं परिग्रहं परिगृह्णाति, षड्भिरुत्तरम्। तद् द्वादशकृत्वः। द्वादश वै मासाः संवत्सरस्य, संवत्सरो यज्ञः प्रजापतिः। स यावानेव यज्ञो यावत्यस्य मात्रा तावन्तमेवैतत् परिगृह्णाति ॥ 13 ॥

ṣaḍbhirvyāhṛtibhiḥ pūrvaṁ parigrahaṁ parigṛhṇāti, ṣaḍbhiruttaram I tad dvādaśakṛtvaḥ I dvādaśa vai māsāḥ saṁvatsarasya, saṁvatsaro yajñaḥ prajāpatiḥ I sa yāvāneva yajño yāvatyasya mātrā tāvantamevaitat parigṛhṇāti // *13* //

सायण भाष्य- पूर्वोत्तरपरिगृह्योर्मन्त्रावयवसंख्यामनूद्य समुचिंत्य प्रशंसति-षड्भिरिति। व्याहियन्त इति-व्याहृतयो मन्त्रावयवाः, ते च पूर्वपरिग्रहे षट्। गायत्रेण त्वेत्यादिकास्त्वान्तास्त्रयः, गृह्णाम्यन्तास्त्रयः उत्तरपरिग्रहे च सुक्ष्मा चासीत्येवमस्यन्ताः षड्व्याहृतयः स्पष्टाः। अन्यत्पूर्ववत्॥ 13॥

Sāyaṇa Bhāṣya- pūrvottaraparigṛhayormantrāvayavasaṁkhyāmanūdya samuchiṁtya praśaṁsati-ṣaḍbhiriti / *vyāhriyanta iti-vyāhṛtayo mantrāvayavāḥ, te cha pūrvaparigrahe ṣaṭ* / *gāyatreṇa tvetyādikāstvāntāstrayaḥ, gṛhṇāmyantāstrayaḥ uttaraparigrahe cha sukṣamā chāsītyevamasyantāḥ ṣaḍvyāhṛtayaḥ spaṣṭāḥ* / *anyatpūrvavat* // *13* //

With six vyāhṛtis (the parts of the Mantras) he draws the first six enclosures representing the northward six tropical movements of the sun during the six months of Uttarāyaṇa, i.e.

a). 23¼° S to 20° S

b). 20° S to 12° S

c). 12° S to 0°

d). 0° to12° N

e). 12° N to 20° N

f). 20° N to 23¼° N and with the six vyāhṛtis, he draws the second six enclosures representing the reverse course, i.e. southward six movements of the sun during the six months of Dakṣīṇāyana period. This makes these together twelve, and thus twelve are made the solar months of the year. The year is the process of the creation. Larger is the yearly process of creation, wider is tropical movements of the Sun between the tropics. So widely, he (the Adhvaryu) thereby encloses this fire altar.

Thus from the aforementioned description of the ritual of Altar enclosure, it is crystal clear that the sun encloses earth at seven tropical lines which are known by the name of seven famous chhandas or circles of latitude.

The diagram given on the next page makes the above description explicitly clear:

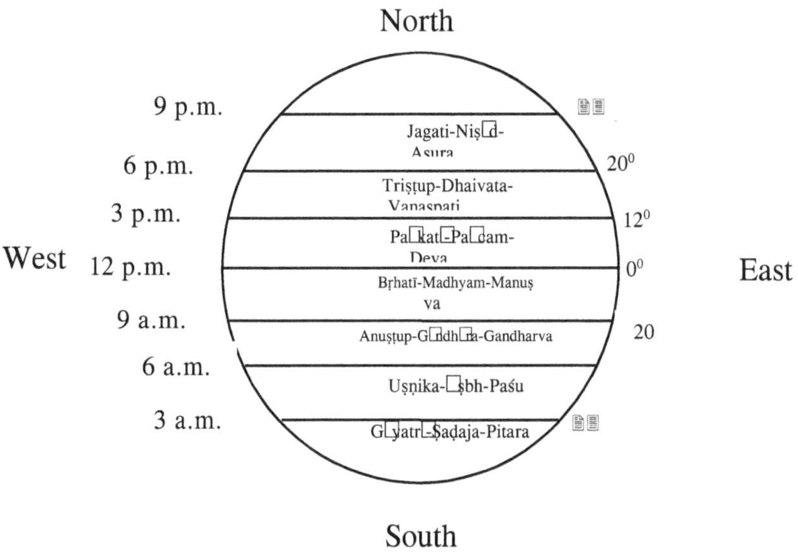

The above-given diagram makes the above descriptions explicitly clear.

These tropical movements of the sun are caused by earth's 23.5^0 North-west inclination on its axis.

Sun's Friendship with Earth: From the foregoing it is clear that the Sun's friendship with the earth is based upon the above seven steps known as 7 tropical movements of the sun in a year. In the other word we can say that the Sun walks seven steps with the Earth in

12 months of the year. Since their natural friendship is based on seven steps, so it became famous in Indian culture that gentle persons can befriend themselves when they walk seven steps together. The famous Sanskrit Poet Kalidāsa expresses this Indian cultural ethos in Kumar Sambhava during conversation of Śiva with Pārvatī.

सतां संगतं साप्तपदीनमुच्यते।
satāṁ saṁgataṁ sāptapadīnamuchyate ।

Based upon this value, a provision of Saptapadī (walking seven steps together) in the marriage ceremony has been made in Indian Śāstrika tradition and so husband and wife are asked to walk seven steps together as they are going to have a nuptial knot for the whole life. Thus the Indian traditions and social rituals are also based upon astronomical phenomenon which is quite scientific.

Here it may also be informed that with the Sun's enclosure of the Gāyatrī chhanda, Uttarāyaṇa, i.e. North or winter solstice commences. The Uttarāyaṇa or winter solstice pointed the beginning of the year. In fact, during the Vedic age, it was also the Devayāna period, due to Indian continent's location being in the Kumeru, i.e. Southern hemisphere of the earth. So the Gāyatrī chhanda has a great significance, being the southernmost point of sun's enclosure on the earth. It was sun's appearance on the earth that caused the emergence of biological life on this planet. In the beginning of the Kalpa, the Gāyatrī cover used to take place in the Makara (Capricorn) sign. These days it takes place in the Dhanu (Sagittarius) sign on Dec. 22.

Keeping in view of the same phenomenon of nature, the documentation of the *Ṛgveda* took place. The

Mantras of the *Ṛgveda* were also composed in seven metres representing the seven parigrahas or enclosures of the Sun on the planet Earth. First is the Gāyatrī metre which consists of 24 syllables thus exactly representing the number of 23.5^0. Since .5 number cannot be represented by syllables, so the no. of 24 has been given to the Gāyatrī chhanda. If we take up the last parigraha, i.e. Jagatī chhanda, we find it just opposite to Gāyatrī, i.e. 23.5^0 N of the equator. Thus the total distance of Jagatī from Gāyatrī is 23.5^0 S to 23.5^0 N, i.e. 24 + 24 = 48. Now one may not find it difficult to understand why the Jagatī chhanda has been given the number of 48. In other words, this is only the reason that Jagatī chhanda consists of 48 syllables. Gāyatrī through Jagatī, there lie five chhandas respectively as Uṣṇika, Anuṣṭup, Bṛhatī, Paṅktī and Triṣṭup. The numbers between 24 and 48 can be divided proportionally into 7 segments each one with an increment of 4 numbers, e.g. 24, 28, 32, 36, 40, 44, 48. As such no. 24 and 48 having been already assigned to the first (Gāyatrī) and last (Jagatī) chhandas, the intervening nos. 28, 32, 36, 40, 44 can be assigned respectively to the intervening five chhandas, i.e. no 28 to Uṣṇika, no. 32 to Anuṣṭup, no. 36 to Bṛhatī, no. 40 to Paṅktī and no. 44 to Triṣṭup. This is the reason why the Vedic seers assigned the above-mentioned sequence of numbers to the various chhandas.

Thus from the foregoing discussion, it is clear that the Vedic metres are not just like ordinary literary metres applied to the compositions of various literary genres. The phenomena of chhanda applied to the Vedic lore has its astronomical base. That is why metres, in the Vedas, have been called as Daivī prajā, or the divine compositions.

छन्दांसि वै दैव्यः प्रजाः ।
chhandaṁsi vai daivyḥ prajāḥ

[Meaning] Metres in the Vedas represent the divine or astronomical phenomena.

As it has already been pointed out above that the chhandas in the Veda are related with the tropical movements of the sun on the earth. So, the first Gāyatrī chhanda represents the first prahara of the day starting at 3 a.m. This is the rising period of the sun. That is why the Vedic seer eulogises the sun through the Gāyatrī Mantra composed in Gāyatrī chhanda. The famous Gāyatrī Mantra reads as follows:

तत्सवितुर्वरेण्यं भर्गो देवस्य धीमहि। धियो यो नः प्रचोदयात् ॥

tat savitur vareṇyaṁ bhargo devasya dhīmahi.
dhīyo yo naḥ pracodayāt

[Meaning] We meditate upon the effulgence of the rising sun, the generator of the world, which is worthy to be meditated upon. This rising sun makes all the living beings swing into various actions."

The above cited 7 cosmic chhandas were used as major chhandas in the documentation of Vedic Mantras. The cosmic latitudinal degrees of the above-chhandas were taken as syllable count for the Vedic Mantras. For instance,

Gāyatrī chhanda has 24 syllables

Uṣṇika chhanda has 28 syllables

Anustup chhanda has 32 syllables

Bṛhatī chhanda has 36 syllables

Paṅkti chhanda has 40 syllables

Triṣṭup chhanda has 44 syllables

Jagatī chhanda has 48 syllables

On the same pattern giving an increment of 4 syllables each, seven more chhandas were formed by the Vedic Ṛṣis. They are as follows:

Atijagati 52 syllables

Śakvarī 56 syllables

Atiśakvarī 60 syllables

Aṣṭi 64 syllables

Atyaṣṭi 68 syllables

Dhṛti 72 syllables

Atidhṛti 76 syllables

Here it may be pointed out that syllable count of the Mantras was not always exactly the same as cited above. We sometimes come across Mantras having one or two syllables less or more than the specified count of the chhandas. We may find Gāyatrī chhanda not necessarily with 24 syllables, it may have 23, 22, 25 or 26 syllables also. Such cases have been given different names. According to Kātyāyana, if a Mantra has one syllable less or more than the specified count of a chhanda, the chhanda will be called Nichṛd and Bhūrik respectively. Thus Gāyatrī chhanda with 23 syllables will be known as Nichṛd Gāyatrī and with 25 syllables will be known as Bhūrik Gāyatrī.

Similarly, if a Mantra has two syllables less or more than the specified count of a chhanda, the chhanda will be called Virāṭ and Svarāṭ respectively. Thus Gāyatrī with 22 syllables will be called Virāṭ Gāyatrī and with 26 syllables as Svarāṭ Gāyatrī.

In addition to the above, we find many other varieties of the chhandas like Kakup, Pada Paṅkti, Vardhmāna, Pratiṣṭha etc. in the Veda Mantras, but they are insignificant.

Metres and their Musical Notes: The Gāyatrī chhanda is pronounced in Ṣaḍaja svara. Gāyatrī chhanda being the sixth one when counted from the Jagatī side, its svara has been called as Ṣaḍaja. This chhanda belongs to the region of Pitaras, 23.5^0 S of equator being known as pitṛ loka. Moreover, the Sun has been eulogized as Savitā, i.e. the creator of the world, similarly the pitaras were the first originator of humanity and the Indian continent tenanting the Southern hemisphere was the first abode of first ever born human being on the Earth. These first human beings were the parents of the rest of human beings. That is why the Gāyatrī chhanda has been associated with the pitṛ-loka, i.e. the ancestral abode or the place of first ever born parents or pitaras. Uṣṇika chhanda, being the second one in sequence, represents the second prahar (watch) starting at 6 a.m. This period is hotter as compared to the period of 3 a.m. Similarly 20^0 South of the equator i.e. Tropic of Aquarius being the hotter region as compared to the Tropic of Capricorn, i.e. 23.5^0 South of the equator. That is why the metre representing the period of 6 p.m. and the region of 20^0 South of equator was christened as Uṣṇika. Moreover, 20^0 South of the equator had the thick forest growth on the Earth. The forest region of the South was known as paśu whereas the forest region of the Northern Hemisphere was called as the vanaspati loka. Due to the dense forest belt, the region was famous as paśu loka.

The Uṣṇika chhanda is pronounced in Ṛṣabha svara. Since this chhanda belongs to the animal world, its svara (musical note) is called as Ṛṣabha.

The Anuṣṭup chhanda, being the third one in sequence, represents the third prahar (watch) of the day starting at 9 p.m. The mid-day time and middle part of the Earth represented by Bṛhatī chhanda are known as a stoma. Since this chhanda follows the stoma chhanda, it is named as Anuṣṭup. This chhanda belongs to the region of Gandharvas. Present day, this region falls in Afganistan and known as Kandahar. During the Vedic period, when Indian continent was tenanting the Southern hemisphere, Gāndhāra used to be located at 12^0 South of the equator. So, the region of 12^0 South of equator was also known as Gāndhāra region. And the musical note for pronouncing Anuṣṭup chhanda was also christened as Gāndhāra.

Bṛhatī chhanda represents the middle part of the Earth, i.e. equatorial region. It also represents the fourth prahar (watch) of the day starting at mid-day, i.e. 12 p.m. So, the musical note assigned to this metre was named as Madhyama svara. Since the equatorial region of the Earth remained densely populated by human beings, this region was known as Manuṣya loka.

Counting Gāyatrī as the first chhanda, the fifth chhanda comes to be Paṅkatī. This is why its name is Paṅktī, the fifth one. The musical note assigned to it is also christened as Pañcam, the fifth one. It belongs to the region opposite to Gandharva loka, i.e. 12^0 North of equator which was geographically known as Deva loka.

From Bṛhatī, i.e. first stoma onward third one is called as Triṣṭup, i.e. the third stoma. Its region is opposite to that of Uṣṇika, i.e. 20^0 North of equator which, being the forest belt of the Earth, is known as the Vanaspati loka. Its svara is Dhaivata. It represents the time period of the sixth prahara (watch), i.e. 6 p.m.

The last one is the Jagatī chhanda which represents the Asura region, i.e. 23.5^0 North of the equator. Likewise, it also represents the 7th prahar, i.e. the period of 9 p.m. Its svara is known as Niṣāda.

All these musical notes are pronounced in various tones depending upon the time period they denote or represent. For instance, Niṣāda and Gāndhāra represent respectively the time period of 9 p.m. and 9 a.m. The number of 9 being the highest one in the series, and the physical energy being at its peak level both at 9 p.m. and 9 a.m., both the svaras are pronounced at the high (udātta) tone. On the other hand, Ṛṣabha and Dhaivata being the representative of 6 a.m. and 6 p.m. respectively or say next one to follow Niṣāda and Gāndhāra in point of numbers, they are pronounced in a low tone or the tone following udātta called anudātta tone. Rest of the three, i.e. Ṣaḍaja, Madhyama and Pañcama being the representative of 3 a.m., mid-day and 3 p.m. respectively are pronounced with the middle tone or mixed tone technically known as svarita tone.

www.ingramcontent.com/pod-product-compliance
Lightning Source LLC
Chambersburg PA
CBHW071807020426
42331CB00008B/2423